A collection
poems insp
by mental
health issues

WE
CAN
DO IT
TOO

Layla Undine

ACKNOWLEDGEMENTS

I would like to thank Joey, my Guardian Angel, for having just as much faith in me as I have in him and assisting me in making my dreams come true. My Nan and Gongey, thank you both for all the love you shared with me during the times when you were still around – I miss you and hope you are both now in a better place. Iris Guy, my best friend, thank you for supporting me when things have spun out of control. I know I'm difficult to deal with. Chloe the Bird, Candyman, Sammy, and all my other friends at St. Andrews Healthcare, thank you for keeping things alive on the ward and making me feel like I'm worthy. Even Dani – Miss Christmas Tree kicker – things have always been up and down with me and you, but I hope we can start afresh. Next time I will knock you out too though, haha.

Andrew Kane from the education department, thank you soooooooooo much for all of your encouragement and excitement – you nearly put me to shame! You really are the best teacher and I may as well say it, in the most platonic and non-scary way, I love you.

Mom, I love you. You are always on the other end of the line, even if I am hard to understand and I sound like I'm talking shit, thank you for listening at least. Dad and Jean, thank you also for helping me in what career I have wanted to do in my life. I know I have switched from one to the other, but I know what I want to do now. I will be a poet. Dad, you said, "Why are you so insistent on making me proud?" Well, it's because I want to say sorry for being an arsehole when I was growing up. That's why. Happy with that answer? Good.

Thank you to everybody at UK Book Publishing too. I appreciate all of your hard work and I have been really impatient, but I now see how worth it the wait was. Thank you all!

To everybody that has bought my book, thank you all for making my dream become a reality. I adore you all!

Layla Undine

ATTENTION IS NOT A BAD THING

"What's wrong, Layla? What are you thinking?"
"You're pacing in circles and clicking your fingers"
I tell them I'm fine and that I don't have any issues
What I really want to say is "Mind your own fucking business"
They're not at all stupid and they know I'm lying
But they leave me alone to cry in silence
I'm too shy to seek attention though they're not realizing
That in my quiet mind I'm feeling suicidal
Why do I withdraw into this bubble?
And how did this come about so sudden?
I want to open up but something's telling me I shouldn't
And now I'm on my own and pushing every one of my own buttons
With everyone else's close observations
They're waiting for me to make conversation
After waiting a few hours I confess my self-hatred
I'm shocked to find that in the end I'm congratulated
I couldn't understand what was good about this
For fuck sake, I just said I want to slit my wrists!
They told me they admired me for my openness
And that honesty is the first step to success
But I thought it was wrong to feel like this, right?
They said seeking help is a form of good insight
At least now someone knows, they are able to support me
And this, kids, is how we all move forward

ATTENTION!

If you scare a skunk you may
Find it's arsehole in your face
Don't be pissed off if it sprays
Because you just dug your own grave

BATTY AND BENCH

We're lion and mane
We're the tiger's roar and
We can talk for hours
Without getting bored

We're tooth and nail
Nobody fucks with us and
We're bucket and spade
Clearing up the sand

We're Batty and Bench
We'll always be mates and
We're joined at the hip
Never separated

We're bowl and pin
We'll make a good strike and
We're dog and bone
We're meant to be united

We're one and one makes one
We're arm and leg and
We're talented spiders
Sharing the same web

We're the open curtains
We're the new revolution and
We're the cure for the itch
We're the beauty of this land

BE MY SHIELD

Secrets lie
They do hide
I must find
The truth behind

Where do I go
To resolve
Painful sorrow
Inside my soul?

Come to me
Pat my back
Wipe my tears
Be my shield

Love me so
More than I do
Create a hole
And dig for gold

Take me away
Far away
To a place
Where I shall be safe

Vow my skin
Shall not be thin
Search deep within
I cannot give in

BIRMINGHAM

UB40 and Black Sabbath
And the USA's most loved accent
The biggest Primark in the world
Let's not forget good ol' Cadbury World
Stefflon Don and her fat arse
As if we ever had to rely on Nicki Minaj
Fish and chippies around every corner
Crazy chicks like my Father's Daughter
Welcome to where we all say "tuth"
We have a football team but they're shit as fuck
Doesn't it feel good to be a Brummy?
Take my hand, Ozzy, let's step forward
Who would want to call their trousers "pants"?
And who would refer to their Mom as "Mam"?
Fuck this shit, it's time to make a statement
Us Brummies shall not be denigrated
You're confusing us AGAIN with the Black Country
Sit down and do your fucking geography!
How are ya, Man? Ennit? Y'alright?
Yeah, sometimes admittedly we talk shite
But for me as a Brummy, born and bred
It's easy to say that Birmingham is the best!

BORN AGAIN

One, two
Hide in my room
Three, four
Shut the door
Five, six
Slit my wrists
Seven, eight
Endeavour the pain

Why am I doing this to myself?
Someone help me with my mental health

Eight, seven
Make me feel better
Six, five
Put down the knife
Four, three
I don't have to bleed
Two, one
Be born again

Now I've calmed down to where I want to be
A psychologist has saved my life for me

Even though she seemed like an obnoxious cunt
All along she had a point
Therapy can be the most annoying thing
But you won't get anywhere denying something's wrong
So speak up for yourself, don't be ashamed
I had to do exactly the same…

…And it's worth the game

DANGER

You bought a smile to my face the day I met you
I knew from that moment I wouldn't forget you
I never realized you'd see me as a danger
I thought you wanted to be mine, I didn't realize you'd hate to
Still, you approached me with such good manner
It's sad to think what did happen after
You talked to me so carefully
Watched every word you said to me
Pointless when inevitably
Your kindness got the best of me
You've captured me and thanks to your theft
In my chest there's nothing left
Why did you have to grab it and flee?
Why couldn't you hold your breath for me?
Maybe I must have scared you off
But I couldn't help it, I'd fell in love
I tried to keep up but I couldn't keep running
In the end I'm left with nothing

DEAR MR. CASANOVA

Dear Mr. Casanova, it's been a while since we last spoke;
this letter is for you being as you blocked me on your phone
What better way could there be to communicate;
in the meantime I'll put your name to shame
We had an argument but you were too weak to tell me why;
you tried to get revenge by ignoring me but it will be you paying the price
You thought that you were dynamite and you took me for a slut;
you even said you loved me, I can't believe I fell for it
I learnt never to judge a book just because it's hardback;
I took another look and now I realize you're an arsehole
Well, I'm glad I got away from you because you are nothing special;
you are a dirty mouthed fool with absolutely nothing to offer
How can you expect yourself to ever get a girlfriend
when your dick is so dead you can't even get an erection?
A year older than me and you're already on Viagra;
give it up, please, what's the point in being a wanker?
Give us the gossip, how many girls are now tripping at your feet?
I suppose you've been talking shit the same way you manipulated me
Once bitten, twice shy and to you I say good riddance;
give it a few weeks and it will be me you're missing
You'd hate to be mentioned in my book of poetry;
that shouldn't matter, you're probably too busy smoking weed
If you found out about this, maybe you would spill all my secrets;
but what kind of man would admit his cock is only six inches?
You couldn't satisfy me, you twat, I'm not even bothered;
you just think you're hard because you're stocky with the same size tits as your Mother
I was attracted to you in early days because I liked how you talked perverted;
yeah, you've had a lot of head but I wouldn't be surprised if you're a virgin
What's wrong? Are you jealous of my recognition and glory?
Or are you just pissed off because at least I know how to go down on a woman?
Come on, now, envy doesn't get you anywhere;
Still, it's normal to be regretful of taking me for a fool
I believe karma is sweet and that it happens to us all;
don't mess with a bitch like me because I'll snap your name in half

DERELICT

Kicked out of my flat because I couldn't pay the rent
Now I'm stealing food from shops and smoking dubbed-out cigarettes
Sitting in the streets of a busy City Centre
An alcohol addiction has made me a prostitute and a begger
Just a teenager from Birmingham, we've never had it easy
I can't afford a cup of tea and my nose and ears are freezing
Pedestrians walk past but they won't look at me twice
Girls like me have no choice but to trade sex in order to survive
Collecting coins from fountains and getting jealous of charities
I have no friends and I've lost contact with my family
Getting hunger sickness whilst I sleep in the cold
Puddles splash upon me from cars speeding in the roads
Why won't someone help me? I've been scrounging here for hours
It's been two days without a drink and three weeks without a shower
So look one more time before you spend cash on fancy clothes
There's kids out there, all alone, with no food or a home

DOMINATRIX

Hello, Mr. six foot tall, are you looking for a cheap ride at all?
Any whore's that take your fancy?
If you wanna be a gimp then you may chance me
Don't be fooled by pretty faces
We all know how to play dominatrix
Something as easy as eating you up could make your entire house corrupt
I've got nails and teeth and whips
Anything to give you your torture fix
I'll blindfold you with a dirty thong, then just make sure you're holding on
'Cos I'm gonna drive you up the fucking wall by barely doing anything at all
Just a little candlewax on your chest
Then fucking your testicles with my breasts
Vibrators on your perineum
I'll make it last until you're screaming
Tonight you are my property
Ain't no prostitutes like me
My blow-jobs are worth a million dollars
Don't worry, I've got more to offer
Kissing your lips and then biting your neck
I'll make sure I leave you with no flesh
I'll rip every hair off of your head
Are you sorry you took a crazy bitch like me to bed?
Tie you face down with leather straps
Claw your back and spank your ass
Whip the behind of your legs
I won't let go until you beg
So you want me to set you free?
Okay, let's roll, that will be eighty pounds please

; -)

DREAMS

I look out the window and watch cars go by
I want them all but I've never learnt how to drive
I look at stars on the television
To beat them all by platinum is my ambition
I stare at houses as I take the bus into town
I dream that one day I'll have two or three of my own
I see jewellers selling diamond rings
I fantasize that I'll have one for every finger
How amazing would it be to be served breakfast in bed?
And to have a gorgeous supermodel girlfriend?
The success I desire is complicated
Not to my closest friends can I explain it
Let me tell you a little secret
All you have to do is believe it
Things like these do not come easy
But if you want it that bad then go and achieve it

FEVER

Here I sit in the middle of January
It should be freezing but me, I'm sweating
I push my feet into the snow
Anything to make me feel cold
The wind blows off my wooly hat
And my hair blows in my face
Car windows are icy
Squirrels are hiding
But the cold I must embrace

Everyone is wearing a hat
And everyone has a runny nose
I am dehydrated
New year is over-rated
I'd do anything to preach wearing no clothes

If only I had a figure to die for
I'd certainly give everyone an eyeful
Strip from head to toe
And dance in the snow
Prove to the world that my nipples aren't erect
Oh, shit these people are strangers, how can I forget? Oops!

FLU

It's a typical and miserable late December
I've got the shits and a bad temperature
I've sneezed what seems like a thousand times
I'm tossing and turning in bed at night
I feel like I've got a frog in my throat
My eyes are watery like my snotty nose
So much for merry fucking Christmas
I don't hear many people listening
All they care about is the presents
Me, all I moan about is the weather
Drinking lemon and ginger tea
With a box of tissues next to me
Doctor, Doctor, help me please
When will this ill health cease?
Maybe I should make a new year's resolution
To agree to take the flu injection

FOUR YEARS

Four years of being routinely debased
Four years of your genitals in my face
Four years of being stunted, you wouldn't let me grow
Four years to be told you're with someone else and you left me all alone
Four years of your lies and your false apologies
Four fucking years of having to listen to Cradle of Filth (Oh, please!)
Four years of being blamed when I wasn't in the wrong
You lived off job seeker's allowance but you never looked for a job
I learnt the hard way and the hard way was from you
I ended up being sectioned for my reaction to your abuse
I'm sorry I broke the law but I'm glad I left you with a scar
That should indicate to all the slags you fuck what a dickhead you really are

GROOMED

It's a new move, I'm finally a step towards out
I'm wondering what this place is all about
I sit down in a new home and the first woman I meet
Was soon to develop an obsession with me
She shows me around and acts like the figure of a Mother
Then reassures me that she will protect me from others
I can't help but have faith, after all she looks tough
Not the kind of woman I'd get on the wrong side of
A few days later she tells me she's in love with me
I'm trying so hard to tread carefully
She smiles and tells me she wants a kiss
Oh, please don't mean that we have to lock lips!
Next thing I know I have her tongue down my throat
I never wanted to be this close
Why can't I stand up for myself?
The truth is I'm too scared of her
Weeks move on and it's in full swing
This woman is sexually abusing me
Caressing my breasts and handling me down there
A so-called bodyguard is my worst nightmare
Crying myself to sleep at night
She won't fuck off no matter how hard I try
Head in my hands now I realize I've been groomed
So frightened I can't even leave my room
I know she's outside waiting for me
So that she can put her dirty hands on me
I wish I could chop all her fingers off
It's the only way all this shit would stop
Come to think of it, I've a new idea
Maybe I should just face my fears
I take a swing at her and she falls flat on her back
What the fuck had I been playing at?
Two fucking years of being sexually abused
And all I had to do was pull my fist out
The alarms go off and I'm dragged into seclusion

At least I can now enjoy my freedom
Still, I couldn't for years tell anyone why I did it
I was too scared that everyone would think I was lying
From that moment on I never saw that pervert
But I managed in the end to confess what had happened years earlier
The sad thing about it is I'll always be a victim
Because I carry such this burden and yet I can't prove it
If it happens to you then please be honest
Because I know how it feels to be a target
The sooner you speak up, you'll protect others too
The world must say no to sexual abuse

HOUSE OF TORTURE

I've always been my own worst enemy
But I never came here to cause any havoc
Next thing I know I'm in a house of torture
No friends, no family or back-up

Put me on a stretch machine
I'll try to be the bigger person
One by one plier all my nails
So I can't bite them when I'm nervous

Place me in the iron maiden
Strike me with electricity
Make me walk on broken glass
With nothing on my feet

Bend me over a wooden table
And hammer nails into my back
Hold my face in a bowl of water
With my hands behind my back

Tie a ligature around my neck
And take me to the gallows
If a miracle happens and I survive
I know you'll try again tomorrow

JOEY

You bring me warmth when it's raining outside. I feel your gentle breath on my face when I was adamant that I was alone. You've taken me under your wing, and through all the noise I still hear you sing. Even when I'm scribbling in books, every drawing regards you. This is love. I promise I shall never run. You are precious. You give me grace. Even when I'm dizzy, you keep me walking in a straight line. Even when I'm blind, I know you'll be my guide.

This is where you, the beauty, looks after me, the beast. This is where we together make two ends meet. This is where you give me a pedestal to stand on. This is where I shall never be abandoned. I feel myself drawn closer and closer to you the more we speak.

Vow you will never leave. Vow you will hold my hand. Vow each other's company. Even when it's time for me to die, I know you'll be in touch. We shall still be a team. There will be no alternative. No substitute. No replacement. You will always be in my heart. I am yours. You are mine.

JUST A LONELY POET

I'm just a lonely poet
I've been detained since I was nineteen
The same four walls surround me
But there's nothing else I need

I'm just a lonely poet
Is there an audience waiting for me?
First I need to show them
That I can make it big indeed

I may be just a lonely poet
But I'm picking up the pieces
I have a lot to prove it
'Cos I'm already in university

I'm just a lonely poet
I sit and dream of bigger places
Maybe one day I'll make it
Maybe one day I'll be famous

I'm just a lonely poet
I've been doing the same thing for years
I've never understood this
Why am I still waiting to be served?

Please somebody pick me up
Please somebody notice me
Please find me somebody to love
Please give me company

Good bye miss lonely poet
Years gone by and dreams came true
I've been refurbished and polished
And now finally I see blue

KS

I shop until I drop
I've got dosh and I won't stop
I've got Ks in my pocket
If I want it then I got it
I used to be a derelict
And now I'm filthy fucking rich
I'm decorated in new tattoos
Check me in my brand name tracksuits
I'm not embarrassed about being ugly
Because at least I've got a lot of money

If I want a set of brand new teeth
I know I can afford it
Bright lights call out to me
Something about being unspoken bored me

So here I am
Get ready for me
I'm putting my modesty behind me

I've heard about the price of fame
Well, I don't know until I taste it
Until then at least I understand being loaded
And with my determination I'll never again be broken

LET ME BE LONELY

Affected again by my personality disorder, and it's come from absolutely nowhere. My mood had dropped and this time I won't stop. Nobody gives a fuck how much I cry, but then I've never really told them why. All I want to do is die. Please, let me be lonely. Don't tell my parents, they'll only disown me. I know you don't trust me anymore, because as soon as I close the door I will get what I have been waiting for. Strip so I'm wearing not a thing at all, then sit alone on my bathroom floor. It's obvious. I apologize. I may not be helping my friends, but you must see that this is how I help myself. Please, let me be lonely. I can't take this any longer. I'll at least leave you with this poem. I want to leave in peace, but not peacefully. It was bound to happen eventually. I am weak. What is wrong with me? I look in the mirror and the fucking glass breaks. I want it. My skin yearns for it. Does this poem give you goose bumps? That's how I've been feeling since I was a teenager. Now I want to tie a ligature. Why not? I've done it before, it's easy. I remember vividly, I was twenty years old and hanging from my bathroom door. Some bastard saved me. At thirty-one, I know I have had enough. DON'T SAVE ME. Let me be lonely. Say your last prayer for me because this time I am going. Going, going, gone.

LIKE CHRISTMAS

The snow is falling down
But it doesn't feel like Christmas
Presents all around
Still, it doesn't feel like Christmas
Where's George Michael now?
Is this really what you call Christmas?
Selection boxes for a pound
What a boring Christmas!

Everybody's got a cold
So it doesn't feel like Christmas
My Nan died eleven months ago
Now I'll never enjoy another Christmas
The local chippy is closed
And it doesn't feel like Christmas
Condensation on the window
But it doesn't feel like Christmas

Everybody's singing
But what's so fucking good about Christmas?
Homeless people are freezing
Yeah, I bet they're loving Christmas
I just can't stop sneezing
And I get this every Christmas
The TV signal isn't working
Man, this doesn't feel like Christmas

Vegetarians and atheists say
"What's the point in Christmas?"
It's just another day
For some reason labelled "Christmas"
Everyone has to pay
Enormous money so kids can love their Christmas
We need more than a holiday
We've had enough of Christmas

LOOKING BACK

You see my name on the shelves and you can't believe your eyes
That's perfectly okay, you don't have to apologize
I understand if you don't remember me
Because I'm not the failure you thought I'd be
You walk further down the aisle and who could it be?
Signing books for the hundreds, yes, it's me!
One of the books is in your hands and you get a little nervous
The queue comes to you and you take a small step forward
What's wrong? Can't you put a name to my face?
Funny I look so different and you're still the same
I've got my grades and now I'm soaking up glory
I used to be a victim now finally I stand taller
If I was to listen to your monotonous bullshit
Guaranteed my life would have been ruined
Look at me, can't you see I'm a fighter?
Nice to see you but I'm surprised you're not retired
If I'm honest I didn't want to write a song about you
Because I didn't want anyone to think I gave a shit about you
Still, it's sweet that you've become a fan
But why did you come crawling back?
Fair, you played a massive part in this success
Because I only grew stronger by ignoring your arrogance
I stand up, reach out and shake your hand
Because looking back I must say thanks
You've made me a superstar
And I'll never forget where I came from
I went through hell my whole damn life
And now I'm enjoying new friends and bright lights

(hope you enjoy my book, dear)

MISERY

It's getting heated in here as my anxiety starts to rise
So I put my boots I'll shake in on and I take a step outside
Lightning strikes above me as the sky gets angry
I smile as I know at least the weather understands me
Thunder roars as loud as I so badly want to shout
I relate to the dark clouds as the rain comes pouring down
I hear people laughing and I want to punch them in the face
I'm self-conscious of their ebullience and I just want to run away
But where would I escape to when the planet is a sphere?
I wish I could fly like lucky birds but gravity keeps me here
I wonder what people mean when they say "reach for the stars"
If only I could get close to one to see how true they really are
I look above and I see little diamonds in the dark
How big are they really and would I have to travel far?
Enough of living in fantasy
I face back down and look at the dirt that surrounds me
I'm sick of this world and what it entails
Maybe tomorrow will be a better day

MISSING YOU

Your demise, it was a shock to the family
What the fuck is happening?
It drove me to insanity
I can't stop missing you

No nicotine is strong enough
No bath water is hot enough
No healing time would be long enough
Whilst I am missing you

I've tried writing all these poems
I've tried therapeutic shopping
I've tried creating loads of drawings
But I'm still missing you

Nobody can talk to me
I keep pushing everybody away
I keep telling the world that I'm okay
But I'm hurting because I miss you

All I'm left with is your green eyes to show
You died when it wasn't your time to go
Nanny, I still love you so
And I'll always be missing you

MOSQUITO

I've never been one for catching a tan
But the heat in the summer was more than I could stand
I innocently thought I could reveal more flesh
And then an evil mosquito bit my leg
Thank fuck these in England aren't venomous
However I was put on a week's worth of anti-biotics
Once bitten (literally) and twice shy
Now I know to cover up when I'm in the sunshine

(Are my poems funny or something?)

MY TOILET

My toilet is living an angry life
It's swallowed too many baby wipes
Toilet I'm sorry
Please forgive me
I promise from now I will treat you right

My toilet won't let anything go down
And it makes a scary rattling sound
Toilet I'm sorry
Please forgive me
I can't bear the thought of letting you down

My toilet was the most precious thing to me
Especially when I had diarrhoea
Toilet I'm sorry
Please forgive me
My bowels can't live without you here

Using a toilet in someone else's room
It just can't compete with a toilet of my own
Toilet I'm sorry
Please forgive me
I'll never betray you again

Is it too late to beg for mercy?
Can't people see how much this hurts me?
Toilet I'm sorry
Please forgive me
Hurry up, I'm bursting for a wee!

NEVER

I never meant to make you cry. I never meant to break your heart. I never thought you cared. I never thought I'd offend you. I never knew you loved me. I never stopped to think twice about my mistakes. I never thought you'd be disgusted by this beast I've become. I never knew I meant anything to you. I never knew you wanted me in your life. I never felt precious to you. I never stepped back and thought about all the stress I was putting you through. I was never on-call because all I cared about was myself. I never patted your back or held your hand. I never felt despondent. I never valued your sympathy. I never wanted to listen to you. I never returned phone calls. I could never cry in front of you. I never hated you. However I never showed affection. I never was grateful. I never let go of my grudge until now. I never met your standards. I never craved your attention. I would never accept I needed it. I never hesitated to denigrate you. I never came home on time. I never cared who I left behind. Was I asleep or was I just never alert?

TOO MUCH NEVER!

I'm sure you wish you'd never looked at this poem. Has it never occurred to you that I have feelings, too? Maybe I never acknowledged yours. Still, this acrimony was never one-sided. I never felt supported at any stage of my life. I suppose I never gave the same privilege to others. I never thought it would take me trying to end my life for you to finally tell me that you loved me.

ONLY

My eyes are only green when they're open (which they always are)
My mouth is only closed when I'm sucking a cigarette
My head only faces down when I'm pulling my socks up
My feet only stop running when I'm walking
My knuckles are only clenched when I'm writing
My hands are only in the air when I'm holding banners
My hair only stands up when I'm cold
My toes only curl when I'm horny
My lips only frown when I've smelt someone else's fart
Nobody can stop me
Only I can stop myself

OVERDOSE

Your love is like an explicit dope
And I've taken another overdose
I'm the luckiest woman you've ever known
And I'm absolutely drugged to the bone

Healthy or not, I just want to get high
I can't fix this obsession, no matter how hard I try
Nobody needs to know what goes on between you and i
But giggling the way I do around you it's hard to hide

Sitting on the sofa with pupils dilated
Why don't we get a little X-rated?
The way you make me feel, I can't explain it
Either way, I'm not complaining

Your generosity is so pure
And believe me, I'm not getting bored
Put your lips on mine and let venom pour
Whilst I take that little bit more

You're so addictive just like a pill
And I won't take anything else to cure my ill
I couldn't give a fuck if this shit kills
So long as I die the way I feel

PATRIOT

I'm a patriotic schizophrenic version
Of Benjamin Zephaniah
I'm equality perverted
And a lesbian on fire

I'm a curmudgeon and an ex-prisoner
And a loyal Slipknot maggot
My poems can be ridiculous
But that too takes talent

I am skinny and ugly but sexy in a way
I can still attract a crowd
I don't care so long as I get my say
Even if I have to shout

Do I have to scream?
I know you can hear me
You choose to ignore me
And I know you abhor me
Because I'm a rock star
In your worst nightmares

PERSONALITY DISORDER

Some people can face
Every waking day
Walking proud and undefeated
Some people can take
Whatever comes their way
Me, I don't find that so easy
Without a voice
Without a choice
All I see is negativity
All is an annoyance
And through all the noise
I'm drowned in my misery
Organic PD
One moment I'm happy
And then I'm anxious and depressed
People surround me
Trying to help me
But I won't let them be my friends
When I finally relax
I try to get them back
But they're pissed off with how I behave
So I withdraw – AGAIN!
When the fuck will this end?
A companion is all I crave
I find myself alone
Wondering how I will cope
So I decide to run a bath
I sit at the side
And cry for my life
Won't somebody please hold my hand?
Soon the water goes cold
I get out, put on my robe
Then pull the bath plug out
When I am finished
I look out the window

If only I could be set free now
But I must face the truth
If I was let loose
Would I still be the same ol' me?
Mental health can be managed
But it shall never vanish
And I can't control my personality
Still look what I have
Despite what I am
My psychosis isn't what I'm based on
One friend is all I need
And I found this in Iris
For now I'll just keep holding on

PERSONALITY DISORDER 2

Sometimes I wake up ready to take on the world and sometimes I feel like shit
So long as I don't look in the mirror when in brush my teeth
I think I can handle it
Sometimes I feel like I am gorgeous and that a model hasn't got a thing on me
Sometimes I walk around with my head hanging down
– please don't look at me
Sometimes I love everyone and even get a high libido
Then on the other hand I won't look at anybody
and won't even masturbate over Dua Lipa (That's saying something!)
Sometimes I'm brave and the wildest fight won't raise a hair on my body
And sometimes I'm scared of the slightest disagreement
even if it doesn't involve me
I sleep with one eye open as I'm always scared of the day ahead
Who is to say whether I will wake up happy or would I rather be dead?
(Truth is, with personality disorder, I think I'd rather be dead)

POETRY AND THE BIRD

One day when I was writing rhymes
A bird landed on my book
She said her name was Chloe
And that she loved my poems
Me, I was dumbstruck!

Not only could this bird read and talk
She also was my fan
Now I know I made it
Because even nature
Is attracted to my pen in hand

The bird said she sees my work as inspiration
And that she has emotional issues
I said "My Darling Chloe
You don't have to be lonely
This poem is for you"

Remember, Birdy, none of us are perfect
I was never born this way
I'm flattered you idolize me
I'll try my hardest to
Encourage you to realize we're two of the same

PRAYER TO MY GUARDIAN ANGEL

Why?
Why do I cry when I am delivered good news?
Why?
Why do I smile when I am in pain?

How?
How can I be grateful for my life after years of suffering?
How?
How can I escape a voice in my own head?

Where?
Where is the light at the end of this dark tunnel?
Where?
Where am I heading to if people say that I haven't yet seen the worst of things?

When?
When will I be set free, if ever at all?
When?
When do I get my act together and put my foot down?

Which?
Which exit do I take when I know they're all dull ends?
Which?
Which way do I turn when I am lost and far from home?

What?
What have I done to deserve this?
What?
What part of me needs to be punished?

Tell me
Tell me why I have to hate myself so much
Tell me
Tell me how I can grow old gracefully
Tell me

Tell me where I can go to find love
Tell me
Tell me when I will be stronger
Tell me
Tell me which direction leads to happiness
Tell me
Tell me what I have to do to be accepted

(prayer in progress…)

Thankyou
Thankyou for making me value myself.
Thankyou
Thankyou for making me feel forever young
Thankyou
Thankyou for giving me peace and love
Thankyou
Thankyou for making me strong
Thankyou
Thankyou for my ability to smile for all the right reasons
Thankyou
Thankyou for allowing others to appreciate me

PREACH

Shoot me for being a martyr
But I won't change my philosophy
So long as I make a point because
Acceptance is all that matters to me
Mental illness has spread a gap
Between me and my family
I love you Mom, I love you Dad
But I can't alter my personality
Maybe you're sick of all these protest poets
I'm here to preach equality
No, in my head I'm not all there but
Don't you dare feel sorry for me
I've had my days where I've wanted to give in
Believed the future had nothing in store for me
Now I'm standing on my own two feet
And writing statement poetry
Why do we have to live in a world
Where all everyone cares about is our criminal history?
Why can't people appreciate us as humans
And give us some fucking liberty?
Nobody is perfect, why can't you see?
We all make mistakes, sometimes regularly
All I crave is just please hear us out
The world must live in unity
Sometimes we can't help being unique but
Rejects are not what we choose to be

PROTEST

For having psychosis, sometimes we get spat on
The discrimination we accumulate in itself is madness
Getting through the stereotype, it's not an easy process
But I know that we are strong and that we won't lose focus
So we sit back, relax and put our feet on the table
It's time to ignore all the jealous haters
Don't listen to all the shit they try to cause us
Because we all know that they're the failures
We may all be individual but we're all ready for a fight
This protest that we make today is clawing for equal rights
We don't need to be sectioned because we're not a piece of cake
It's about time that we all as one had chance to liberate
We won't let others underestimate us because we are still breathing people
We may have some issues but we don't deserve a label
We walk proud regardless and we shall not be defeated
If haters don't like the truth then they can pick up my shit and eat it

REDEEM MYSELF

Months have gone by and it's time to be honest
This could be a letter or a poem
There are just some things I need to say
Because I'm fed up of carrying so much hate
I'm sorry for the songs I've written
I'm sorry for my passive-aggression
I know I've been a bitch
There's no denying it
I've been selfish and two-faced
I've hurt people more than backache
No drug could cure the pain I've caused
I don't even know what I did it for
My greed and my envy
It didn't get me anywhere
I kept laying fuel on people's patience
Just to see what I could get away with
I knew all along
That what I was doing was wrong
If you're willing to let me
If it means anything
I'd like to redeem myself
Yes, I need to redeem myself
Please, let me redeem myself
If only I could redeem myself...

RIHANNA REMIX

The perfect woman exemplary
Was to be mine for only temporary
But every time I look at her face I see
Her beauty still resonates with me

We tried our best at such a devoted pace
Knowing we found love in a hopeless place
For this we had to close this case
And put a handsome future all to waste

An amazing friendship not condoned
So we ended up despondent on our own
The thought of living all alone
Still makes me shiver to the bone

Two hearts not broken but they were stretched
From one long distance to the next
Tell me how I can get out of this net
Then lay this obsession down to rest

Restrictions caused us to separate
Now I feel like I'm aching, bruised and grazed
Though I must take all this pain to my grave
My fondness for this woman will remain

SCAPEGOAT

It's one of those days, there's no ambience in this room
I push everyone away and then I'm left on my own
Why am I furious at everyone else for my loneliness?
Scapegoating them all when it's only me that caused this mess
Why can't I admit that it's me that's hiding?
I spend hours, days and weeks living in denial
I've always been keen to avoid putting my name to shame
I'd much rather find another person to blame
I need a helping hand but I'm just too proud to ask
I view crying as weakness so I do so behind people's backs
Sometimes I'm too scared to even show my own face
So I lock myself in an empty room that slowly becomes a cage
These tears do fall but there's nobody to wipe them
I want to approach somebody but I'm too frightened
It's shocking, really, how much I withdraw
Then assume it's what everyone else is guilty for
I've lied so much by now, I should have learnt my lesson
As history repeats itself it doesn't make me feel better
What privilege do I get from trying to frame someone else?
I guess it's easier than having to put duress upon myself
I don't know why I bother, It doesn't even affect them
Because the truth is it's only me that carries such this burden
I can't confess and I won't confide
I can't even look anyone in the eyes
I'm a fraud, I'm a liar and I'm a cheat
It's pointless putting trust in me
I say I'm comfortable but I just need some space
And then I throw it all back in their innocent faces
What kind of friend do I work out to be?
Nothing that comes out of my mouth is real
Be wary of me – I'm quick to point the finger
When nobody else has done a single thing wrong
I'm foolish and too pompous to apologize
Well, now I'm full of enemies and I'm not at all surprised

SECOND BEST

He went out smelling like roses
Then he came back smelling like coke
What has happened to my soulmate?
This is not the man I know
I'm getting wary of him
And I don't want to get too close
A part of him is missing
Because I know that he is stoned
I manage arms-length distance
But he can't put his arms around me
I'm scared to even kiss him
So I peck my fingers and touch his lips
Tears fill my face
As I know this man is broken
If I wasn't a good enough addiction
Then why couldn't he just be open?
I can't believe I'm second-best
I feel like I've been mugged
All I wanted was to be his Princess
But I was beaten by a drug
He falls asleep and we lie back-to-back
I can't help myself but grieve
Why can't anyone understand
What this man is doing to me?
I'm kept awake all night
By his coughing and his snoring
I'm not surprised he's tired
After spending the previous evening snorting
I suppose it doesn't matter how I react
There's fuck all I can do for him
I suppose I just have to face the facts
To this man I mean nothing

SELF-DESTRUCTIVE

Pacing around in circles and wearing baggy clothes
Waiting for text messages on my phone
Watching the clock, when you will be home?
I miss you

When I'm not with my best friend I become self-destructive
No appetite or will to do anything constructive
There's nothing out the window but I can't stop looking

Nobody can fulfil me when you're not around
Nobody can lift me when you're not around
But we've shared more secrets than I can count
I miss you

When I'm not with my best friend I become self-destructive
Negativity overwhelms me and I just can't function
Sitting in utter silence until I finally hear the doorbell
Then I get to see the best friend I've ever had in my lifetime!

SO MANY TIMES

So many times I've lost my way;
I've always wanted to speak but not known what to say
So many times I've tried to end my life;
wanted to scream but telling myself to be quiet
So many times I've tripped and fell;
running too fast for fear of being hit below the belt
So many chances I've been given to start a new chapter;
ignored it all and now it is too late to go back
So many times I've walked away, leaving good times behind;
I was too ungrateful and inpatient to store them in my mind
So many hours I waste whilst I dwell on the past;
Hating the failure and weakness that made me who I am
So many poems I've written with my heart on the pages;
Just another song to represent all I've hated
So many words of advice that didn't match my ambition;
Now and then I get reminded but though I'll never learn my lesson
So many rules I've broken and fucked with the law;
now paying the price as I can't be trusted any more
So many times I've tried to apologize;
but it's futile because nobody will take my side
I'm sad for the embarrassment I've caused my family;
but it's no surprise when you consider the calamity
I'm sorry Mom, I'm sorry Dad;
for the waste of a daughter that you once had

SOMEBODY LIKE ME

You make me feel gorgeous
You make me feel VIP
All because somebody like you
Wants somebody like me

You make me feel like number one
You make me feel so sexy
All because somebody like you
Wants somebody like me

It was a match made in heaven
You knew that I was keen
I can't believe somebody like you
Would want somebody like me

I never had much of an ego
I had so much insecurity
I can't believe somebody like you
Could want somebody like me

You could do so much better
You've got people tripping at your feet
Still you insist every day
You want to be with somebody like me

A girl too shy
To wear her heart on her sleeve
Still you're only interested
In being with somebody like me

There's just no comparison
Between you and me
How could somebody possibly
Want to be with somebody like me?

I would fall to pieces
If you ever left me
Somebody like you is needed
By a lucky somebody like me

STORY OF MY LIFE

All my life I've been a curmudgeon
My opinions have made me the judged one
I have never been one to idolize
It took me thirty plus years to realize
Though being victimized all my days I've held a grudge
Seeking revenge like I did works for not one
Neither me or they acknowledged that nobody was perfect
Still I was trampled upon and I didn't deserve it
By thirteen I was seeing a child psychologist
The posters on the wall I spoke to were the only friends I had left
I carried so much hatred inside until I lost the plot
Ended up slitting my wrists but satisfied I was not
Left home when I was fifteen and was homeless a year later
Prostitution was for myself the only way I could cater
Wrote letters to my Father saying he was a shit parent
Got involved in knife crimes like I was careless
Started drinking booze until I was addicted to the substance
Was sectioned and admitted to rehab within an instance
I flirted with staff and got involved in sexual activity
Became a pathetic narcissist when I met people jealous of me
I was denigrated for my homosexuality
And my psychosis meant everyone had a problem with me
Twenty years old and I'm caught hanging off my bathroom door
At that time I wished I had never even been born
I could never be in the crowd for the way I dressed
And the music I listened to hardly impressed
So I got frowned on for having piercings and wearing spiked collars
Nobody wants to know you when you're a mosher
Regardless, things improved and I went to low secure
But I was groomed by a woman almost the moment I walked through the door
I spent two years blaming myself for that predicament
I thought I shouldn't have been so sexually disinhibited
I thought maybe me acting provocatively
Gave her the impression that she was welcome to me
I know I've spent so many years acting like a baby

Kicking off when things haven't gone my way
But what exactly did ever go right?
This is only a brief summary of the story of my life
My Grandparents passed away and I'm still grieving
I had inheritance and now I'll never be loved for the right reason
Still I'm grateful for all this has educated me
Motivated me into university
It's time to turn my life around
I've been lifted; I just hope I don't come crashing down
I have dreams of standing up and making speeches
To inspire individuals with mental illness
I can speak for all when I say we just want to be heard
Give me everybody's number, I'll speak to the world
But please forgive me for things I've done, I'm only human
Everybody has a history and I'm still a person
Looking back there's no such thing as irrational
Because my mental illness has made me a champion

TAKE AWAY

It's our lucky day of the month
Damn, we have to go to morning meetting
All the patients start to argue
Over Chinese, Indian or pizza

After what seems like ages, boy did we feel it
Now it's all served on our plate
Eat it up, yum! A little wait
Now it's time to defecate!

Sit down (on the bog, that is) and let it all flow freely
Like your bowels would demand
Squeeze out every little poop
Just make sure you wash your hands!

TASTE IT

Everybody has hopes and dreams
Do you think I could be famous?
If I truly throw myself out there
Maybe one day I could taste it

I used to be homeless on the streets
And now I have too much money
Could I cope with stardom consequence
If I had paparazzi upon me?

To see my face in the newspapers
Wouldn't that be reassuring?
My name could be mentioned on the radio
So often that it bores me

Is celeb world what it's made out to be?
Let me in for a day
But if I'm impressive enough for them
Then I guess I'd have to stay

TEDDY IN MY BEDDY

Little teddy
In my beddy
Gets no sleep at night
All my snoring
Tossing and turning
And my farts give him a fright

But he has energy enough
To give me a hug
When I need a shoulder to cry on
Little teddy
Oh so caring
Whether I'm anxious, sad or frightened

Little teddy
How do you do it?
You take all the pain away
You're so fluffy
Come to Mummy
Let me hold you if I may

Little teddy
Always ready
Waiting patiently for a cuddle
Little teddy
He always tells me
Don't be afraid of thunder

Little teddy
In my beddy
Try to sleep, my darling
Little teddy
Tries to beg me
"Then stop your fucking farting!"

THE CANDYMAN

Bow down to the Candyman
In the sun she'd catch a tan
Armed with her Gay Pride band
If a man wanted her she'd say "Have a wank"

All hail the Candyman
She gave me ten pairs of brand new pants
She walks around with a fancy swagger
And always has me in fits of laughter

Let's salute the Candyman
She really is a handsome lass
All it takes is a hug and she cracks my back
And it makes me horny when she grabs my ass

Standing ovation to the Candyman
Never intimidated, she's always got a plan
Hulk Hogan? Nah, she'd batter that
Not to mention the "Camel grab"

Remember only the Candyman can
In three hours she smokes eighteen fags
We make a perfect duo as I sing, she farts
She really is a work of art

THE INDONESIAN OWL

Be cautious, it's the Indonesian owl
It hears you from behind and turns it's head right around
The bird representing death with it's eyes orange and round
When it hears a rat it comes soaring down

The fright
He might
Does he bite?
Look at the size!

Be wary, it's the Indonesian owl
It can see you even if you don't make a sound
The height of him, he should wear a crown!
I'm so scared of the big Indonesian owl

The fright
He might
Does he bite?
Run for my life!

TO BE HEARD

I've spent years in the system
And I'm tired of being ignored
So shut up for a minute and give me chance to talk
You keep categorizing the ill
What are you doing that for?
Can't you see we're laughing back at you
Because your shit smells just as raw?
We're sick of all your slights
You're just making our ears sore
One person had to make a statement
And it's my name that was called
Things are going to change today
It won't be like what it was before
If you think I'm soft as roses
Then be wary of the thorns
You're judging what you don't understand
And now we're getting bored
Don't even try to pity us
Mental illness doesn't make us poor
If you can discriminate what you don't know
Therefore there is no cause
It's time somebody stood their grounds
Because we won't condone this any more
Challenge me, I'll win the fight
I'm ready to pull out swords
When you realize we have just as much strength
You'll fall flat to the floor
I suffer with psychosis but I'm not a psychopath
So don't try and stereotype me at all
I may have instability
But I'm still powerful to the core
You try so hard to move us to one side
I don't know why you even bother at all
You need more than words to defeat us
Because this crowd isn't small

Denigration won't hold us back because
Regardless we stand tall
We must follow what's in our hearts
And not tolerate any more cruel
Years ago with prejudice
We'd curl up into a ball
Be ashamed of ourselves and tears would fall
Until we couldn't cry any more
Now we have faith and are motivated
To see what dreams are for
All this negativity must stop
We mustn't feel like we've been torn
I've idolized poets that write art against inequality
And that they do perform
I've gained enough confidence in myself
And I'll be doing just that for sure
Hopefully with my voice being heard
My honesty will be the cure
So thank you to my open-minded audience
A new revolution has been born

TO MY FATHER, TO MY DAD

To my Father
I remember how it used to be
I could never believe that you loved me
We separated
I was glad to get away
I used to think that house was a palace of hate
You sent me a letter
Sealed it with a kiss
I knew then it was time to forget this shit

To my Dad
I see how it is now
All I want to do is make you proud
We've accepted each other
Joined forces and united
I can't believe all the years we've wasted
Such animosity
I held a grudge
And now I'm willing to be your Princess

I love you, Dad
You and your wife too
I guess my only option now is to prove
That I'm a woman
With a beautiful family
These resentful thoughts have stopped chasing me
It was my childhood
That made me who I was then
But what's important is only who I am today

xxxxxxxxxx

TOO LATE

Oh, no
I've drank too much coke
Oh, no
I start to choke

Oh, no
My head starts to hurt
Oh, no
My stomach turns

Oh, no
My ears are popping
Oh, no
I can't stop burping

Oh, no
My eyes are watering
Oh, no
I feel like vomiting

Oh, no
I'd better run quick
Too late
I've already been sick

TRIP TO THE DENTIST

Too many sweets and now I have toothache
A dental appointment has been made
Maybe I need a filling here and there
That's what I like to think, wait until I'm there

I take a seat in the waiting area
Dreading what lies in store for me
Reading posters on the wall
Trying to be distracted then my name is called

I walk into a room so very tiny
So this is where the sadists have been hiding
One shakes my hand and greets me with a smile
Tells me to lie down, relax and open my mouth wide

He looks at my teeth and starts to talk in a strange language
I'm scared as I know only the other sadist understands it
Wriggling a metal implement against my tender gums
I wish I could just run away because I know this won't be fun

Sadist says I need fillings, as if I haven't enough already
He asks me if my toothbrush is manual or electric (yes, it's electric)
Then he tells me I will be put under anaesthetic
Oh no, not again, now I'm going to be injected!

Just as I consider leaving
He tells me my wisdom teeth need removing
What part of being a dentist does this man enjoy?
See how he likes it, I'll break his jaw (not really)

Well, in goes the needle – ouch! You bastard!
He assures me the pain won't be everlasting
What the fuck, I can't even feel my lips!
Why couldn't he inject me when i COULDN'T feel it?

So he's finished and I'm left with fillings and two less teeth
He tells me I have to wait an hour until I can eat
A little while later I feel dizzy and sick
That's just the shit you get when you're on anaesthetic

Kids! Don't eat too many sweets!

TWO HAIRY TOES

I haven't shaved in a week or so
And now I have two hairy toes
Where are the razors?
This is disgraceful
My feet have been abandoned
And now they're in demand
But what about my legs?
Shouldn't the pubes be there?
And what about my pits?
There's no excuse for it
So out comes the shaving foam
Say Goodbye to hairy toes

UNLUCKY THIRTEEN

It's a late Christmas visit, you're flattered with kisses
Opening presents and getting fed
It's been an amazing day and I know you're tired
I think you need to shoot home and rest

Go to bed early, sweet dreams for the night
Then get up for the daily routine
Time for biscuits and a cup of tea
I'm soon to find out what "thirteen" means

The staircase that took an old lady's life
I wish I could tear the carpet off of them
Please Nan, wake up, how can this be?
I beg those green eyes to open

Looks like you've fallen asleep for good
Because of a cruel and unexpected demise
A bullet that hit the family happened
Thirteen days after Christmas time

It kills me more than it killed you to know
That you passed away in panic and pain
But after losing a fight with an ugly game called life
I hope you're in a better place

UNSCATHED

I could never pull my hood up far enough
I just wanted to hide my face
I'm sure I looked like I was a thug
But myself I was taught to hate

I spent years of my life
So consumed with jealousy
I listened to everybody else's slights
And let words get the better of me

If your butt was bigger than mine
I would be absolutely gutted
I'd point blank refuse to exercise
And stuff my face with junk food

I'd plaster my face with make-up
Rocking wigs and wearing false nails
It's not like I wanted to be a model
But I was never completely unscathed

So the world thinks I'm ugly
But is this really the most important thing?
Self-efficacy doesn't come easy
So long as you're not your own enemy

Don't vilify yourself
You're just making yourself a victim
Look after your mental health
And fuck everyone else's opinion

WAIT FOR ME

You own me
You own me
Your support is the first step to my success
Don't kill me
Don't kill me
Before I have chance to prove myself
Please hold me
Please hold me
I promise I won't run away again
Fulfil me
Fulfil me
I'll always hold on to what you said
Trust me
Trust me
Why won't you hold another breath?
Wait for me
Wait for me
You know I'll get there in the end

WHEN...

From good fortune you were sent
"Lean on me" is what you said
All I can do is relent
Because I know that when...

When the streets get violent
Guns and knives cause silence
I know that you'll find me
And take me out of hiding

When the heat starts to rise
And anger builds inside me
I know deep inside
I have security from your kind

When I'm feeling lonely
Finding it hard to stay focused
That's when you overdose me
With company so devoted

When I'm lying naked
And my whole body is shaking
I know that you'll save me
To you I am wholly faithful
When all I can do is crawl

And I have no voice to talk
I know you'll be on-call
When the rain begins to fall

When cars are crashing
And windows are smashing
Everybody has lashed out
But I know you won't back out

When everyone's too drunk to care
Sharing needles and throwing chairs
I know of course that you'll be there
With reassurance to share

When children are getting hurt
And books are getting burnt
When beggars aren't getting served
You have power to cure this curse

When I'm thinking I should give in
When I'm thinking I can't do this
When I'm thinking my life is ruined
My mood by you is lifted

Thankyou Prince Charming
You know who you are
A friend like you is all I've wanted
A pure soulmate and more

YOUR MAJESTY

To help me see blue when I'm dressed in grey
To help me look forward to the following day
To teach me to fly without looking down
To help me to swim when I was scared I'd drown
To help me bounce back when I'd hit the ground
To encourage me to turn my misery around
To keep me on my feet and motivated
When I thought I wasn't appreciated
Now I see what true friends are for
After so many years of being ignored
You bring me light in a long, dark tunnel
When I feel the dust and webs upon me
Your majesty, the Queen of hearts
I thank your Mother for her work of art
Maybe it's serendipity
That I met you and you met me
If it wasn't for where we both reside
This everlasting bond I would not find
Just as I was about to give up
I looked one more time and there you stood
What is this masterpiece before me
The start of a friendship's eternal story
The more we find we have in common
The more I begin to believe in heaven
Whoever has created you, they've made no mistakes
Because you are perfect in every way
Your sense of humour
Your honesty
Your beauty and your loyalty
Thank you for helping me off my knees
You'll always have a friend in me

(Dedicated to Iris Guy)

Printed in Great Britain
by Amazon